from BLESSING *to* BLESSING

THE CATECHISM AS A JOURNEY OF FAITH

SEAN INNERST

ASCENSION PRESS

West Chester, Pennsylvania

Published by Ascension Press
Post Office Box 1990
West Chester, PA 19380
Customer Service: 1-800-376-0520
www.AscensionPress.com

Cover design: Devin Schadt

Printed in the United States of America
11 12 13 14 15 16 7 6 5 4 3 2 1

ISBN 978-1-935940-12-8

To the Glory of God, Father, Son, and Holy Spirit,
through the immaculate hands of Mary, and
for my dear wife, Catharine, and the beautiful
children she has given me: Patrick, Brigid, Mary
Catharine, Gabriel, and Elizabeth Mae.

St. John the Baptist and St. Augustine, pray for us!

God, the Blessedness, in whom and from whom
and through whom all things are blessed, which
anywhere are blessed ... Thee I entreat.

– *St. Augustine of Hippo,* Soliloquies, *1.3*

Contents

Acknowledgments. vii

Foreword. ix

Introduction 1

Chapter One:
From Blessing to Blessing 9

Chapter Two:
God Has a Plan. 27

Chapter Three:
The Economy of Salvation. .39

About the Author 59

Acknowledgments

I would like to thank my colleagues at St. John Vianney Theological Seminary and the Augustine Institute for their support and patience while this work has been geminating and now, finally, sprouting. Special thanks have to go to my shepherd and spiritual father, Archbishop Charles J. Chaput, OFM Cap., as well as to my Rector at the seminary, Msgr. Michael Glenn, who has made time available for me to work on this and other catechetical projects.

Foreword

It is only with the passage of time that wine reveals its complexity and nuances. As a teacher of the *Catechism of the Catholic Church*, I have found that this most important of books in the Church has the same quality. Although many Catholics have read at least part of the *Catechism*, few have grasped its real value as a catechetical tool. With the passage of time, however, the genius of the *Catechism* as a tool for introducing people to Catholicism and for giving Catholics a better understanding of their faith has been borne out.

Having presented the *Catechism of the Catholic Church* many times to adult students from eighteen to eighty, I am convinced that it should not be consigned to our bookshelves as a kind of Catholic fact book we pull down and dust off every so often to answer doctrinal questions. As Blessed Pope John Paul II noted upon its publication, the *Catechism* is intended to be "a sure norm for teaching the faith."[1] With apparent unction, the Holy Father also shared his hope for the *Catechism*, "May it serve the renewal to which the Holy Spirit ceaselessly calls the Church of God, the Body of Christ, on her pilgrimage to the undiminished light of the Kingdom!"[2] While this may have happened in small pockets of the Church, few would say the *Catechism* has yet to truly renew the Church as a whole.

This sad reality is not the *Catechism's* fault. It is a remarkably

---

[1] John Paul II, Apostolic Constitution *Fidei Depositum* (1992), 3.
[2] Ibid.

rich compendium, elegantly structured and beautifully written. Even a cursory glace at its pages reveals that it is not a stale book of dogmatic "facts" at all but rather a precious map or guide to the Christian journey of faith. Read in this way, it effectively serves the purpose for which Blessed John Paul II prayed.

Many begin to read the *Catechism,* find it difficult, and give up. With a little coaching, though, what at first seemed impossible becomes not only doable but enjoyable. Once its themes are grasped, the *Catechism* helps us see our Christian journey—and our Catholic identity—in an entirely new way.

The purpose of this book is to explain the intention and themes of the *Catechism,* so as to make its content more accessible. It is intended to serve as a reading guide, if you will. It adds nothing to the *Catechism;* it is only intended to help others appropriate it better. Here are some of the ways it can be used:

- To prepare for personal reading of the *Catechism*

- As a catechetical instrument for RCIA or adult education classes

- As a manual for seminarians studying the *Catechism* at the beginning of their seminary training

- As an introduction to or general instructor's manual for the *Pillars: A Journey through the Catechism* catechetical program

- To highlight the guiding themes of the *Catechism* while using the shorter *Compendium of the Catechism of the Catholic Church* text for content in adult education or RCIA classes

My great hope is that what this booklet presents will lead others, as it has led me and my students, to a deeper faith, hope, and love of God in the very Marian heart of the Church.

– Sean Innerst

Introduction

The Christian faith can be thought of as a journey. The foundational documents of Christianity, the Old and New Testaments, are essentially stories of the human journey from sin to salvation. The *General Directory for Catechesis,* the Church's manual for catechists, also tells us that, when done properly, "catechesis takes the form of a process or journey," what it later calls an "educative journey."[3] So it shouldn't surprise us that a catechetical work of the Church such as the *Catechism* should aim at getting the larger biblical story of the journey of mankind to God to coincide with our personal stories in such a way that we can see them as one story describing one journey.

And so, the journey theme expressed in the subtitle of this text, *The Catechism as a Journey of Faith,* ought not to be thought of as a *mere* metaphor to describe our Christian lives. Catholicism is not just a body of propositions or "faith facts" to be learned; it is a life-long journey that one undertakes in faith. There are certainly vital doctrines that we hold as Catholics, and the *Catechism* is very much taken up with disclosing these. But our faith is directed toward a Person, Jesus Christ, whom we profess to be the Way, the Truth, and the Life.

---

[3] *General Directory for Catechesis* (Washington, DC: United States Catholic Conference, 1997), nos. 143, 147.

In the Holy Spirit and through the fullness of revelation in the Son, God the Father is known in truth. But the Son came to reveal him, not simply so that we might *know* that God is Father, but so that we might *go* to live with him in heaven forever. This is what we mean when we say that the Son is not only the *Truth*, but the *Way* and the *Life*. This book, based upon the content of the *Catechism*, seeks to emphasize the way and the life of faith so that the truths of faith that the *Catechism* teaches might be understood and embraced more fully.

The *Catechism* asks us to begin to live it in a new way, to undertake a journey to a new land of freedom and truth. It asks us to make new commitments to the love of God and neighbor in answer to the call of Christ as it has echoed down through the centuries in the one, holy, catholic, and apostolic Church he founded. This introductory text is an implicit invitation not only to read the *Catechism* and to study its contents, but also to participate more fully and deeply in the sacraments, to live the moral teachings of the Church more faithfully, and to commit to an active love of God in prayer. And, of course, this invitation to a faith which is professed, celebrated, lived, and prayed is the very same invitation that the *Catechism* itself offers in its four pillars.

It is essential to note at the outset that this journey is not something that any of us can undertake on our own. It can only be undertaken in the grace that comes to us from the Father, in the Son and Spirit. Be assured that those who have undertaken this journey are blessed for having done so. You will be, too.

Although the *Catechism* itself is the map of this journey, and it is only by reading it that you will see the terrain in its precise details, it is important that we have a rough idea of the general route of the journey before beginning. That is what this short book is intended to provide—namely, a clear description of the point of departure, the path, and the destination of the journey the *Catechism* describes so that we can undertake it with confidence. These are expressed in the *Catechism*'s use of three important themes: the *blessing*, the *plan*, and the *economy* (or history) of salvation. As we will see, the theme of the *blessing* is both the starting point and destination of our journey, while the themes of the *plan* and the *economy* provide the path between the two.

God is Our Origin and Destination

Before beginning a journey, a traveler needs to consider three things: the starting point, the destination, and the route or path between the two. The *Catechism* supplies us with most of what we need to know about all three in its opening sentence, which reads, "God, infinitely perfect and blessed in himself, in a plan of sheer goodness, freely created man to make him share in his own blessed life." That, in a nutshell, is the whole journey; in fact, it is the whole story of time, and the cosmos, whose duration it measures. The general pattern of the journey of faith can be clearly seen here.

First, there is but one **starting point** for the journey and one goal or destination, and they are one and the same. Everything that is or has ever been has come from God, who this first sentence of the *Catechism* describes as "infinitely perfect and blessed." And everything that is or has ever been will return to him. Those things that are not possessed of spirit will find a different sort of resolution in him than those of us who are spirit, who think and will freely. Those of us who are spirit will be divided in the end into those who have loved, believed, and hoped in him—and so can live with him—and those who have not—and thus cannot.

The *Catechism* tells us from its very first words that our journey is one from "blessing to blessing." We come from God and we are going back to him. The only difference is whether we go willingly! Heaven is our rightful home, but God forces no one to enter it. The goal of a Christian is certainly to "share in his own blessed life" forever in heaven, but even those who have no such ambition must appear before God at the end of this great and universal journey. So, the pattern of all things from the very beginning until the end of time has always been the march of everything from "blessing to blessing." Thus, God is both our starting point and our destination.

The Plan for the Journey

The second great facet of the journey is linked to the first: Not only are our starting point and destination clear, but there is a clear path to follow. This path is disclosed as a *plan*, a "plan of sheer goodness," as the very first sentence of the *Catechism* describes it. This word "plan" appears repeatedly in the *Catechism* to indicate the Father's saving will for the human race. God's desire is for all men "to be saved and to come to the knowledge of the truth."[4] This saving will of God is carried out in the Son, the face of the saving plan of God.

In the first chapter of John's gospel, he is revealed as God's *Logos*, a Greek term meaning "word," but which can also mean plan, pattern, or reason. The Incarnate Son of God expresses in himself, and in all his works and words, the path back to the blessing of the Father.

The Plan in the Economy of Salvation

The third facet that needs to be understood before engaging the *Catechism* is the *economy of salvation.* (Here, the term "economy" is used in its ancient Greek sense of "stewardship" or "management of a household" rather than in the modern sense of economics.) This refers to God's plan of loving goodness as worked out in human history. This history is a chronicle of man's successes and failures, of men and women cooperating or not with God's plan, a plan that is only fully revealed with the coming of the Word made flesh, Jesus Christ. The "economy" is the working out of God's

---

[4] 1 Timothy 2:4

saving plan in history, from the creation and fall to Christ's Second Coming in glory.

Just as the journey we have been discussing has three facets (the blessing, plan, and economy), the path of the journey through the economy has three phases:

- From the Father's open hand comes all of creation and the promises of the Old Covenant,

- through the Son's Incarnation and saving death comes the Redemption of the human race, and

- from the work of the Holy Spirit comes the sanctification of the saved.

This is the great story which we are moved to enter and make our own by the Holy Spirit who authored it. And this story, planned in the Son and effected in the economy by the Spirit, is also the path of our journey.

The Journey in the *Catechism*

These three facets or themes of the *Catechism*—the *blessing*, the *plan*, and the *economy*—form the basic matrix from which springs its doctrinal teaching. This doctrinal teaching is presented in the four parts or "pillars" of the *Catechism*:

I. *The Profession of Faith* (the Creed)

II. *The Celebration of the Christian Mystery* (sacraments)

III. *Life in Christ* (morality)

IV. *Christian Prayer*

Although categorizing the content of the faith in these four groupings is time-honored in the Church's catechesis (see Acts 2:42), the *Catechism* is clear that the Catholic faith should be thought of "as a unified whole" (CCC 18). The emphasis upon the way God's plan to draw us to himself is fulfilled in the great human journey from blessing to blessing is one way the unity of content is maintained in the *Catechism*. Thus, the *Catechism* reminds us that Christianity is the story of a journey, a journey that we may embark upon, once we understand and enter that story.

The four pillars, far from being just subject divisions, are related to the story of salvation: 1) The Creed (*The Profession of Faith*) is the summary of the story; 2) the sacraments (*The Celebration of the Christian Mystery*) reenact and bring the story alive; 3) the moral life (*Life in Christ*) is the way in which we make the story our own; and 4) The life of prayer (*Christian Prayer*) is the way we surrender the authorship of our personal stories to God as we grow in our relationship with him. So journeying through the *Catechism* is a way to learn to read, understand, and enter into the true story of God's plan to bless us.

This great narrative—framed by the blessing of the Father and his plan in the Son and worked out in history at the prompting of the Spirit—has a particular plot. This plot becomes clear when we read this universal story with the Church who has been instituted by God to tell it.

The True Story of Our Journey

Towards the end of his gospel, Luke gives us the story of two disciples on a journey from Jerusalem to Emmaus.[5] Their hopes that Jesus was the Messiah have been tragically disappointed. Suddenly, they are greeted by a mysterious stranger who asks them to tell their story.

The two disciples describe the great works and words of Jesus, his conflict with the Jewish authorities, and his passion and death. They even relate that some women had reported a vision of angels and that his tomb had been found empty. They have all the facts right, but they apparently cannot put all the pieces together in a meaningful way.

---

[5]   Luke 24:13-35.

The mysterious figure fascinates them with a retelling of that story "beginning with Moses and all the prophets," demonstrating that "the Christ should suffer these things and enter into his glory."[6] Their hearts burn within them as they hear the whole economy or biblical story retold by this figure that they finally recognize as the risen Christ when he breaks bread for them.

In this way, Jesus teaches them the Church's doctrine of salvation by telling the saving story of prophecy and fulfillment in the economy—the same story the Church continues to proclaim today. This is the Gospel story that the *Catechism* tells, and out of it percolate all the doctrines that serve as guides to us on our journey from blessing to blessing. Knowing the plot of that great story we can learn to read our own story in light of it and begin to walk in the same way that the disciples did.

The disciples on the road to Emmaus, having heard the story told rightly and recognizing the risen Christ as the fruit of it, go immediately back to the heart of the Church, the gathering of the apostles in Jerusalem, to confirm what they have seen. They are able to reenter that fellowship because they can now read their own experience within the larger story that Christ has shown them. Their journey away from Christ and his Church has been halted and reversed by the divine story that the Risen One tells them. They are able to reenter the apostles' fellowship because they can now read their own experience within the plot of the larger story.

The Doctrine of the Story

The doctrines of the Church taught in the *Catechism* can be thought of as the "grammar" of the story. They help us understand what the words of the story mean and how they stand in relation to one another. But it is possible to know the grammar without having heard the story. It is only by the proper telling of the story itself that the value of these truths comes into view. The doctrine and

---

6   Luke 24:26-27

the story go together—and the *Catechism* makes sure we get both by embedding the doctrine of the Church in this great story of the journey from blessing to blessing. Thus, it helps us to see not just *what* the Church teaches, but also *why*—that is, how each doctrine fits in the story. When the story is rightly told and seen as our journey of to God, then we can be moved by grace to undertake our part in the great migration of all things back to the Father.

In the following chapters, we examine the three major themes that frame the story the Church proclaims about the Triune God who made us, saved us, and who continues to work to make us holy so we can return to him in glory. Whether you know it or not, you are already part of that story. My hope is that this short book, *Blessing to Blessing*, will help you read this story rightly so you might enter into it with your whole mind, soul, and strength.

Chapter One

From Blessing to Blessing

"God, infinitely perfect and blessed in himself, in a plan of sheer goodness freely created man to make him share in his own blessed life." (CCC 1)

The Map for the Journey

As we have already seen, the opening sentence of the *Catechism* is a seminal description of the whole of history, from its origins in God to the end of time when he will draw all things back to himself. God's plan stretches from eternity to eternity, from blessing to blessing.

As the *Catechism* tells us, "Blessing is a divine and life-giving action, the source of which is the Father; his blessing is both word and gift."[7] In the ancient world, the blessing of one's father was much sought after. We can see this in the struggle between Jacob and Esau for the blessing of their father Isaac in Genesis.[8] The *Catechism* goes on to say, "When applied to man, the word 'blessing' means adoration and surrender to his Creator in thanksgiving."[9] So the Father, the font of life, is the origin of all blessing, the first of which

---

[7]   CCC 1078. This phrase implies that the Father blesses us by way of the Son ("word") and Spirit ("gift"). Remember that his plan in the Son is worked out in the Holy Spirit in the economy.
[8]   See Genesis 27.
[9]   CCC 1078

is that he has willed us into existence. We are further blessed when
we return this blessing by surrendering ourselves to God in adoration and thanksgiving, both in this life and forever in heaven. That
is the rightful purpose of every human person. The blessing is our
beginning, our point of origin and our destination.

In this movement out of and back to God, from blessing to
blessing, man is cast at the center of the drama. He is the free
object of God's free decision to allow him to "share in his own
blessed life." Why, of all creatures, is man so central to the great
sweep of history? It is because without man, there is no history.
Neither angels nor animals write history, even though they figure
in it. History is solely the story of the human race.

According to the *Catechism,* man is not simply the center of
history; he is the center of creation itself. *"Man is the summit* of the
Creator's work,"[10] and is "the only creature on earth that God has
willed for its own sake."[11] Christ, the God-man who comes at the
center of human history to effect "his saving plan," makes man the
summit of creation, "for in him all things were created in heaven
and on earth, visible and invisible."[12] Angels, animals, and man
were made in, through, and for the God-*man.*

Man stands at the summit of creation because of his creation
in God's image and likeness—and because of the Incarnation.
God not only humbles himself in this remarkable way, he asks the
angels to imitate him by serving us. Man is the center of the story
because the story expresses God's "saving plan" *for* man.

Neither the animals nor the angels can be saved. The animals,
while suffering with us some of the effects of original sin, do not
bear the taint of it. They are simply what God has created them to
be and they give him glory by being that. The angels, on the other
hand, were given free will, but each, at some point after their cre-

---

[10] CCC 343.
[11] CCC 356.
[12] CCC 331, quoting Colossians 1:16.

ation, fixed their wills for or against God. As we will be after death, having decided either for or against God, they are now.[13]

God "desires that all men be saved and to come to the knowledge of the truth,"[14] but he doesn't force the issue. Man is at the center of the story because he is at the center of the conflict between good and evil. This journey upon which we are engaged is a perilous one, both because of its uncertainty and because of the forces that are arrayed against us: the fallen angels, as well as our own weakness. We need a guide along the way back to the Father. Christ himself is our Way, Truth, and Life. As God, he is also the origin, reason, and end of our journey. He has given us the Church, "the pillar and bulwark of the *truth*"[15] to aid us as the primary guide on that journey. The *Catechism* is a *true* map of the *way* to reach our destination.

The *Catechism* is not merely a "book of Catholic facts" or a compendium of Catholic beliefs. Our journey toward the blessing of eternal life with the Father depends less on what we *know* than on what we choose to *do*—or, even better, on the way we choose to go. Christ is the Truth God reveals, but that Truth must become the Way if we are to reach the Life he promises. So while the *Catechism* represents a "sure norm for teaching the faith," as Pope John Paul II declared, it serves us best if we treat it less like a fact book and more like a roadmap for our journey to God.

All maps contain a "key" that explains their symbols. We could say that the three themes we have previously described function as the key to the map. So let's open the map and examine the key a little more closely in preparation for the journey.

---

[13] See CCC 392–393.
[14] 1 Timothy 2:4.
[15] 1 Timothy 3:15.

Our End is in Our Beginning

Every journey has a destination. In fact, all human activity is oriented to some sort of goal, whether a place or a state of being or some other.

The journey of faith is no different. Its destination is heaven. Since God is an infinite and eternal Spirit who lives outside of time and space, our destination is not a place but a state of being that the *Catechism* calls "his blessed life."[16] The *Catechism* presents this goal in its very first paragraph because without a clear destination or goal, we cannot really begin our journey.

St. Thomas Aquinas said that "the end is the rule of whatever is ordained to the end,"[17] by which he means that the goal influences all the acts employed to gain it. If we make an evil outcome our intended goal, everything we do to get there will be colored by that evil goal. If we choose some good end as our goal, all we do will be colored by that good. Of course, having a good end doesn't guarantee that all the means we choose will be good. We can choose either a good means or an evil means to a good end: I can rob a bank to feed my family or get a proper job. In both cases, the acts I take to attain the end are, as St. Thomas says, "ordained to the end," though one of the means (i.e., robbing the bank) is obviously evil.

Having a clear sense of where we want to go is especially important in our journey of faith because, unlike the example just given, we cannot choose an evil means and attain the blessed life of God in heaven. All evil means will point us in the opposite direction. In this sense, the destination of our lives exercises a much greater influence on us than does the goal of a physical journey. On our spherical globe I can set off to the east or west and, while the two journeys will be very different, I can still arrive in the same place. But if I set off on a determined course for heaven or for hell, toward

---

16 "This perfect life with the Most Holy Trinity—this communion of life and love with the Trinity, with the Virgin Mary, the angels and all the blessed—is called heaven" (CCC 1024).

17 St. Thomas Aquinas, *Summa Theologiae*, I-II, 1, introduction.

God or away from him, the two journeys *and* destinations will be very different. We need to know the end of our life's journey; the more we know about and desire heaven, the more heavenly will be the way. We have to know that we have been made for a blessing to make our lives blessed. And a blessed life will lead to a blessed end.

Our Destination is also Our Happiness

Having recognized that any journey requires a clear destination, and that our destination on the journey of faith is the blessing that is God, let us now consider a little more closely the blessing he promises. We can see that the Father's intent in creating us was to enable us to "share in his own blessed life."[18] Most of us who are (or desire to be) religious persons are accustomed to thinking of our religious search or journey in terms of fulfilling God's will, of living in accord with his intention for our lives.[19]

The *Catechism* makes it clear that, contrary to popular opinion, God's claim on us is not opposed to who we are. God is not a cosmic dictator who demands our allegiance and obedience under threat of arbitrary punishment. One of the great gifts we have received in Christ is the revelation of God as loving Father. In fact, God's desires and those of our hearts match. The Father only wills for us what we truly want. As the *Catechism* says, "The desire for God is written in the human heart, because man is created by God and for God; and God never ceases to draw man to himself. Only in God will he find the truth and happiness he never stops searching for."[20]

A life lived in accord with God's will is not entirely one of delayed gratification. God wills and works to effect our happiness at every moment. The *Catechism* quotes Psalm 105, "Let the hearts of

---

[18] CCC 1.

[19] The *Catechism* recognizes the claim that God exercises upon his creatures by stating that "at every time and place, God draws close to man. He calls man to seek him, to know him, to love him with all his strength" (CCC 1).

[20] CCC 27.

those who seek the Lord rejoice."[21] That is, we do not have to wait for heaven to rejoice in the Lord. We can do that at any moment—if we live in his grace and are mindful of his love.

The *Catechism* says, "The desire for God is written in the human heart." The heart, as spoken of here, is the deepest part of us. That place where we are most who we are, you might say. At this deepest level, man is clearly "a religious being."[22] But this fundamental orientation of man, this essential part of who we are, "can be forgotten, overlooked, or even explicitly rejected."[23] Whether by sin or ignorance, we often forget who we are and what we are looking for. We look for the happiness that only God can provide in wealth, honors, power, or beauty. While these things, because of their origin in God, can give us some measure of happiness, they cannot satisfy the deepest desires of our hearts.

More than Happy ... Blessed

Aristotle (384–322 BC) describes happiness as the fullest development of our highest human powers—i.e., the intellect and will—over our lifetime. He meant that when we fill our minds with truth and our wills with goodness, we become the people that we are naturally meant to be.

The Father has revealed in Christ that our minds and wills are made still happier—in fact, supremely happy—when they are filled with him, with the blessed life that he is. That graced or supernatural happiness is called "beatitude" (from the Latin *beatus*, which means "blessed" or "blessed one"). This is not a passing happiness that comes from created goods, and it is even more than Aristotle's happiness of right thinking and acting. The happiness that God wills for us is the beatitude (or graced happiness) that can

---

[21] CCC 30.
[22] CCC 28.
[23] CCC 29.

come from allowing our minds to be filled with his truth and our wills with his goodness.

These wonderful blessings are ours for the asking. But although God supplies that which we cannot do ourselves, he asks for our cooperation. The *Catechism* tells us, "This search for God demands of man every effort of intellect, a sound will, 'an upright heart,' as well as the witness of others who teach him to seek God."[24] Our journey toward God requires that we work to make our own the blessing that the Father gives freely. Jesus enjoined us to "strive to enter by the narrow door; for many, I tell you will seek to enter will not be able."[25] The happiness that God promises is free, but it doesn't come cheap.

The search for happiness is a major theme in the *Catechism* because it is a major theme in our lives. Everyone seeks happiness. Rather than pushing us toward heaven from behind by religious injunctions or dictates of God's will, the *Catechism* aims to draw us forward toward the very destiny we most desire. The *Catechism* doesn't *demand* a faith response from us; rather, it *invites* a response of faith in love and promises us happiness in return. We might think of the *Catechism*'s presentation of the faith as a wedding proposal from God himself, who wants his bride (the Church, i.e., us!) to be eternally blessed with him for all eternity in heaven (see John 14:1-3).

If we decide (under the workings of his grace) to accept God's invitation, we may start now the journey to the wedding feast of heaven (see Revelation 19:7) in the full certainty that the destination of that journey is the fulfillment of everything we desire. As the *Catechism* says, "Heaven is the ultimate end and fulfillment of the deepest human longings, the state of supreme and definitive happiness."[26]

It is important to note that this sort of invitational appeal is

---

[24] CCC 30.
[25] Luke 13:24.
[26] CCC 1024.

what makes the *Catechism* a different sort of catechesis. We could call it a new catechesis for the New Evangelization. It is not just a rehashing of "old stuff," as some might think, but an invitation particular to our age. The "stuff" in the *Catechism* is indeed "old"— it is the ancient Tradition of the Church—but its editors recognized that "old stuff," even if of great value, doesn't always attract us moderns as it ought to. For good or ill, we want to know what is in it for us.[27]

Thus, the *Catechism*, from its very first words, presents us not merely with the story of salvation, as a way of avoiding hell (as this truth might have been phrased for earlier generations) but also with beatitude—the graced fulfillment of the heart's deepest longings. Rather than simply describing the content of our faith as earlier catechisms have, the *Catechism* suggests that this content ought to appeal to our hearts as well as our heads. Both head and heart must be engaged in a full, human embrace of faith, and in the *Catechism* head and heart work in concert in a number of ways.

One last note on happiness: We may initially undertake the journey simply to be happy, and this is sufficient as a beginning. As the philosophers tell us, happiness is that thing for which all other things are sought. Everything that we pursue in this life we pursue because we think that gaining it will make us happy. Once we have gained some spiritual maturity on the journey, we come to recognize that our true happiness is only found in God, not in a purely selfish search for it. Maturity in grace teaches us that God, not merely our own happiness, is the real purpose for the journey.

God alone is the primary reason to do anything—so, if you want to be happy, pursue God. Later, you will find that only pursuing God will make you happy. This is why Jesus can ask us to take

---

[27] In 1983, Pope John Paul II called for a "New Evangelization," describing it as new "not in content but in its ardor, new in its methods, and new in its means of expression" (*Address to the Bishops of Latin America* [CELAM, March 9, 1983], III, AAS 75 [1983] 778). In just this way, the *Catechism* presents the enduring content of the Gospel in a new method and with a new ardor.

up our cross daily and follow him while at the same time promise that it will be light and easy. Real love may not always make us happy in the sense that we used this term as children, but adults know that real love is the source of the deepest form of happiness. That is the reason that Christ can promise us both the cross *and* happiness in following him.

As we have already noted, before beginning a journey a traveler needs to know three vital things: the starting point, the destination, and the route or path between the two. Here we seem to have discovered a fourth necessary element: our reason or purpose for going. As it turns out, on this journey the blessing is not only our starting point and destination, but also the reason or purpose for undertaking it. God is our origin and end *and* the very reason for the journey. As the ultimate answer to the human search for happiness, he calls us out on to the road of faith that leads to him.

The Blessed Trinity and the "trinity" in Us

If we are to receive this graced happiness that we call blessedness or beatitude, we need to allow our highest powers (i.e., intellect and will) to be perfected by grace, by God's truth and goodness. This is the journey to which the *Catechism* invites us. We should also consider a third human power, the memory, which St. Augustine saw as representing the third of a trinity of powers in the human soul. Augustine saw that each of us image the three Persons of the Trinity by the three powers in our souls: memory, intellect, and will.[28]

Augustine posited that the intellect represents the image of the

---

[28] Christoph Cardinal Schönborn, general editor of the *Catechism*, has noted that the "psychological analogy" of St. Augustine that we are employing here was not included in the *Catechism* because it is expressive of just one theological evaluation of the way in which the human person images God and so is not specifically catechetical. By including Augustine's very helpful theological tool I don't intend to try to import a theology into catechesis, but to highlight the *Catechism's* Trinitarian mode of catechesis.

Son in us, who, as the Word of God, is the Father's perfect conception of himself. The will images God the Holy Spirit in us and is the seat of our ability to love, just as we speak of the Holy Spirit as the love between the Father and the Son. The *memory* is the foundation of the exercise of our other powers, just as God the Father is the foundation of Trinitarian life, the Person from whom the Son and the Spirit proceed. That is, to think with my intellect or choose with my will, I must be able to remember what I want to think about or choose. We could even say that my thinking and willing proceed from my power of memory, just as the Son and the Spirit proceed from the Father. And so, according to Augustine, we have a trinity of powers in our souls that reflect the Trinitarian life of the God who created us.

If our highest powers—intellect, memory, and will—must be perfected for us to reach our goal of graced happiness or blessedness, we might expect God to offer some sort of spiritual help so we can attain that perfection. That is in fact just what he does. This help to each of our highest powers is reflected in the various sections or "pillars" of the *Catechism*.

Three-fold Grace for Our Three Powers

First, the intellect, which is brought to perfection by faith, is given the content of the faith in the first section of the *Catechism*— the Profession of Faith. This section on the Creed is a summary of what God has revealed. All that he has revealed finds its perfection in the coming of God's Son into history.

Recall that Augustine associated the second Person of the Trinity, the Son or "the Word," with the power of intellect in us. Thinking about what God has revealed is the first step toward the renewal of our minds in Christ that St. Paul urges us to begin in Romans 12:2. When we reflect on the Creed we see the "plan of sheer goodness" that the Father has disclosed in Christ to bring us to blessedness.[29] The Creed, then, is a brief description of the *plan*

---

[29] CCC 1; see also CCC 257.

of the blessing as it has been worked out in history. It is the plan of the blessing in miniature. By assenting to God's plan, the intellect is blessed, or brought to perfection in grace.

The next human power is the memory, which is perfected in connection with the virtue of hope. The second pillar of the *Catechism*, which focuses on the sacraments of the Church, holds the clue as to how God helps us to reach perfection in hope. Paragraph 1082 of the second pillar tells us that the blessing is both "revealed and communicated" to us through the sacraments.[30] First, the plan of blessing is *revealed* in the words of Scripture read in the Church's sacramental liturgies. Then, the blessings the Father promised in Scripture are fulfilled for us in the present as they are *communicated,* or given to us, through the grace of the sacraments.

In the sacraments, our recognition that the Father is faithful to his promises is joined to his fulfillment of those promises in grace. In this way, we are given both the reason for hope and, through grace, the power to hope. Recall that Augustine associates our memory in a special way with the Father. It is our "remembering" of the Father's faithfulness to his promises in our sacramental celebrations that enables the memory to be the instrument for our perfection in the virtue of hope.

Finally, the will, the third of our trinity of powers, is perfected by charity. This process is reflected in both the third and fourth pillars. The third pillar concerns the moral life and the fourth teaches about prayer. Since the will is the seat of our ability to love, Augustine associates it in a particular way with the Holy Spirit. The Beatitudes and the Ten Commandments describe what Christian love or charity looks like in action. The Beatitudes, in particular, describe the "blessed life" to which God calls us, even in this life. It is the graces and gifts of the Holy Spirit we receive in the sacraments that enable our wills to be perfected by actions in accord with the Beatitudes and Commandments.

---

[30] CCC 1082.

The journey toward the blessing that is God himself is begun in us by faith in the Creed, advanced by the hope for salvation granted us in the sacraments, and in the charity expressed by a morally upright life of beatitude. Charity then reaches its height in us when we give our wills over to God in that act of love which is prayer. In fact, the attitudes expressed in the Beatitudes can only really be understood, appropriated, and practiced by someone who prays. It is by prayer that one develops a hunger and thirst for righteousness, for poverty, for real repentance.

As we read in the *Catechism*, "Blessing expresses the basic movement of Christian prayer ... prayer of blessing is man's response to God's gifts: because God blesses, the human heart can in return bless the One who is the source of every blessing."[31] Prayer is the blessing received and given in return. Prayer is also the way we turn the authorship of our stories over to God. When we pray, "Thy will be done," we surrender our will to his and he begins to lead us on the journey of faith in a new way.

A Trinitarian Structure

We see, then, that the life of faith described by the *Catechism* promises our intellect, memory, and will (the trinity of powers that St. Augustine recognized as reflecting the image of the Blessed Trinity) the blessing of a trinity of virtues (the theological virtues of faith, hope, and charity) to aid us on our journey back to the primordial Blessing which is God himself. These Trinitarian associations are illustrated on the following chart.

---

[31] CCC 2626.

The Holy Trinity of Divine Persons	The Trinity of Human Powers	The Trinity of Virtues	Parts of the *Catechism*
Father	Memory	Hope	Sacraments
Son	Intellect	Faith	Creed
Holy Spirit	Will	Love	Commandments and Prayer

This profusion of threes (three Persons, three powers, three virtues) is no accident. As the *Catechism* says, "The mystery of the Most Holy Trinity is the central mystery of Christian faith and life. It is the mystery of God in himself. It is therefore the source of all the other mysteries of faith, the light that enlightens them. It is the most fundamental and essential teaching in the 'hierarchy of the truths of the faith'."[32]

Since the Trinity is the "central mystery of Christian faith and life," it is not surprising that the *Catechism* follows a trinitarian structure when presenting the content of that faith and life. Although the *Catechism* has four parts (and there is an important

---

[32] CCC 234.

reason for this),[33] many of the internal divisions of those parts are by threes. For example: the Creed and the sacraments each are divided into three parts, the moral life is perfected by three theological virtues, the revelation of prayer is disclosed in three ages, etc. This trinitarian structure indicates, first, that the faith is ordered in itself and so subject to arrangement by category and theme, and, second, that it is so because it has been given to us by God who is Order itself and a Trinity of Persons.

Father

Holy Spirit   Son

Eternal Beatitude with the Holy Trinity in Heaven

↑ Prayer –
                                    Charity in the Will
↑ Moral Life –

↑ Sacraments –   Hope in the Memory

↑ Creed –   Faith in the Intellect

↑ The Journey of Ascent in the CCC

Memory

Will   intellect

Body

---

[33] In Hebrew thought, the number three was the divine number, a symbol for God or the things of heaven, because the Hebrew superlative form of the adjective, the "best" of anything, was formed by repeating the adjective three times. That is why we still say of God that he is "Holy, Holy, Holy" to mean that he is the Holiest. The Jewish symbolic number for the things of earth was four, as in four directions, four winds, four seasons. We could say, then, that in the *Catechism* where God is imaged in some way we find threes, and where our earthly journey is concerned we find fours, as in the four pillars of our earthly journey of faith.

Conclusion

In its four pillars, the *Catechism* offers us what we might call an *itinerary* of faith, a plan to follow on the great journey from blessing to blessing. This blessing is at the same time our origin and our goal. It is none other than the Blessed Trinity, Father, Son and Holy Spirit, who has created us, redeemed us, and who wills to sanctify us in a "plan of sheer goodness."

It is important to note that every stage of this journey from blessing to blessing is itself part of the blessing that we call Christian faith and life. In other words, the blessing does not come only when the goal is attained; it is an integral part of the journey itself. God wants us to be blessedly happy both here and hereafter and the very structure of the four pillars suggests that.

The Creed is a summary of the plan that God has for our blessing; the sacraments are the places where that blessing is fully revealed and communicated to us. Having been blessed with the saving grace that comes through the sacraments, we can then undertake a life of obedience to the Commandments, leading to that fulfillment in beatitude which we see expressed in the Beatitudes. And, finally, the life of prayer draws us close to God by way of a reciprocal blessing in which God blesses us and we bless him in return for all that he has done. Behind all of this lies the perfect love that the Blessed Trinity has for us. By the gifts of faith, hope, and charity, the Father's aim is to draw us into that perfect union of love that is the beatific vision of heaven.

The *Catechism* is a precious map for this journey back to our blessed Beginning and End. And Christ, who was sent by the Father to issue this invitation to his "Father's house," is himself the key to the map of our journey. He is, in fact, the invitation itself; as the *Catechism* says, "the Beatitudes depict the countenance of Christ and portray his charity."[34] He is the very picture of the blessedness to which we all secretly aspire and to which the *Catechism* calls us.

---

[34] CCC 1717.

He is the perfect Son of the Father, the icon of what it means to have received the Father's blessing.

Final Blessing

In paragraphs 1077 through 1083, the *Catechism* presents a short but powerful discourse on the blessing, beginning with the beautiful hymn from Ephesians 1:3-6: "Blessed be the God and Father of our Lord Jesus Christ, who has blessed us with every spiritual blessing in the heavenly places." Here, St. Paul blesses God the Father for the supreme blessing that he has given us in Christ. In this sublime hymn, we see just a little hint of the way in which we will bless God the Father for all eternity in that superlative meeting between the Blessing that he is and the blessing in return to him that we will then be.

"Blessing" or "beatitude" in the *Catechism*: A Sampler of Texts

Pillar 1 – Creed

CCC 184: "Faith is a foretaste of the knowledge that will make us blessed in the life to come" [Quoting St. Thomas Aquinas]." (See also CCC 1, 59, 148, 257, 336, 962, 1009, 1024.)

Pillar 2 – Sacraments

CCC 1079: "From the beginning until the end of time the whole of God's work is a blessing. From the liturgical poem of the first creation to the canticles of the heavenly Jerusalem, the inspired authors proclaim the plan of salvation as one vast divine blessing." (See also CCC 1078, 1080, 1081, 1082, 1360, 1671.)

Pillar 3 – Moral Life

CCC 1718: "The Beatitudes respond to the natural desire for happiness. This desire is of divine origin: God has placed it in the human heart in order to draw man to the One who alone can fulfill it." (See also CCC 1717, 1719, 1721, 1722, 1723, 1731, 1855, 1934, 1949, 1950, 1975, 2090, 2548.)

Pillar 4 – Prayer

CCC 2626: "Blessing expresses the basic movement of Christian prayer: it is an encounter between God and man." (See also CCC 2589, 2627, 2645, 2676, 2781, 2803.)

Chapter Two

God Has a Plan

"Through an utterly free decision, God has revealed himself and given himself to man. This he does by revealing the mystery, his plan of loving goodness, formed from all eternity in Christ, for the benefit of all men." (CCC 50)

A Plan of Blessing

The term "plan" is used more than a hundred times in the *Catechism*, so it is clearly an important theme to its editors. We live in a time when the providential care of God is often doubted, when various ideologies suggest everything in the universe is meaningless or the product of a random series of accidents. With this worldview, we can begin to think of *ourselves* as accidents. The *Catechism* wants to stress, therefore, that the exact opposite is true.

We, and everything else in creation, are willed by the Father. He had a "plan," formed from all eternity, to bring us into being and to draw us, in love, toward the Blessing that he is. Because God's plan for us is rooted in his love, it does not force us into cooperating with it. God does not force salvation upon us but offers us its benefits along with wonderful proofs of his loving providence in Sacred Scripture: "From the beginning until the end of time the whole of God's work is a blessing. From the liturgical poem of the first creation to the canticles of the heavenly Jerusalem, the inspired authors proclaim the plan of salvation as one vast divine blessing."[35]

So, as we have previously seen, the first thing that we have to recognize about the plan of the Father is that it is a plan of blessing— or, better put, a plan for *our* blessing. It expresses the Father's intention to bring us the blessing that he wills for us. As we will see, the basic pattern of God's plan is Christological and ecclesiological, meaning that it comes to us through Christ and his Church.

As the *Catechism* tells us, "Blessing is a divine and life giving action, the source of which is the Father; his blessing is both word and gift."[36] That word is embodied in the God-man, Jesus Christ. In him, we have the "fullness of all revelation."[37] We sometimes repeat such phrases without recognizing their *full* meaning. How is Jesus the "fullness" of God's revelation? When we say that Christ is the full revelation of God we don't just mean that Jesus, as he appeared during the thirty-three years of his earthly life, was supremely full of information or that he said more about God than anyone else. While he did possess all the fullness of wisdom and knowledge (see Colossians 2:3) and, as St. John the Evangelist tells us, all that he said and did couldn't be contained in all the books in the world, Jesus is the "fullness" in a still "fuller" way.

In his letter to the Ephesians, St. Paul says that God "has made known to us in all wisdom and insight the mystery of his will, according to his purpose which he set forth in Christ as a *plan* for the fullness of time, to *unite* all things in him, things in heaven and things on earth."[38] We should first note from what St. Paul tells us that Christ is the expression of the Father's "plan," and that this plan is in accord with his "will" and "purpose."

Second, the purpose of that plan is to "unite all things in [Christ]." In Greek, the word translated as "unite" is *anacephalaeosis*,

[35] CCC 1079.
[36] CCC 1078.
[37] CCC 65, citing *Dei Verbum* 2.
[38] Ephesians 1:9-10, emphasis added.

which in other Scripture translations is rendered "sum up" or "recapitulate." This difficult word (and the theme it expresses) has been commented upon by many important Christian teachers, beginning with St. Irenaeus of Lyon in the second century, and mined for what it tells us about Christ.

Here, St. Paul is not only saying that the Father intends to unify all things in Christ but also that Christ is the full disclosure of the Father's plan for the whole of human history. Christ is the *unifying principle of all things*. He is the reason, the goal, and the center of the whole human story.[39] And so, as St. Paul puts it, Christ is the summation of all things.[40]

Knowing this, we begin to see that the full doctrine of Christ is really more than that he is the Incarnation of God. He is also the preexistent Word, or *Logos*. He is God from all eternity and that Person of the Trinity about whom we say in the Creed, "through him all things were made."

At the Incarnation, we see in Christ the plan for all things, that is, God's "will" and "purpose." Christ is everything that the Father has planned for us from before time. He is the very portrait of the blessing that God wishes to bestow upon us. It is in this sense that he is what the *Catechism* calls (echoing St. Augustine) the "whole Christ," the *Christus totus*.[41] Elaborating on St. Paul's description of the Church as the Body of Christ,[42] the *Catechism* can say that together the head (Christ) and the members (Church) make up the one Christ. They are one Body, just as a husband and wife are one body.[43]

The *Catechism* makes clear, however, that Christ is united not just with the Church as it now exists on earth. Indeed, he and the Church throughout history are one, until the end of time. The

---

[39] See CCC 450.
[40] Ephesians 1:10.
[41] CCC 795-796.
[42] See 1 Corinthians 12.
[43] See Ephesians 5:30-31.

Church was, in one sense, born at the Cross, but the "plan born in the Father's heart" was "already present in figure at the beginning of the world."[44] So the *Catechism*, quoting two ancient sources, can say, "The world was created for the sake of the Church" and "the Church is the goal of all things."[45] This is quite a bold statement!

One might say that in some mysterious way, the Body of Christ was already present in the world before Christ took a body.[46] This body was being prepared in the time of the early patriarchs and in the history of Israel for its eventual full disclosure and completion in Christ. Thus, if the "whole Christ" is Christ joined to the Church, and the Church includes "all the just from the time of Adam, 'from Abel, the just one, to the last of the elect',"[47] then the "whole Christ" spans the whole of human history.

The Whole Plan

We live in a world that often denies the ordered quality of history. Many of our contemporaries believe that there is no order or purpose to the world or to human life itself. Some believe that God (if he exists at all), either through indifference or impotence, has abandoned the world he created to the vicious tendencies of human striving. Many today are implicit *deists*, seeing God as an absentee landlord who really doesn't much care what we do or interfere in our affairs in any significant way.

The ideologies of our age have worked to convince people that blind chance is behind everything and that we are all accidents. You and I might never have been, and nothing of any consequence would be changed by

---

[44] CCC 759.

[45] CCC 760, quoting the Shepherd of Hermas and St. Epiphanius.

[46] St. Augustine if Hippo expresses this in a wonderful section of his work *Instructing Beginners in Faith*, using the example of the birth of Jacob in which his hand, which had grasped the foot of his twin brother, Esau, protruded from the womb before the rest of him: "And in an analogous manner, the Lord Jesus Christ, previous to his appearing ... sent before him, in the person of the holy patriarchs and prophets, a certain portion of his body" (Chapter 3, 6).

[47] CCC 769, quoting *Lumen Gentium* 2

our absence. This is called *nihilism*. It is the disease of modern meaning-lessness. When people are gripped by it, life becomes empty of purpose and we tend to focus on our own pleasures and aggrandizements. We either become wholly selfish or grasp at vain political or social programs by which to make the most of an otherwise hopeless situation.

The *Catechism* is intended to be a frontal assault on modern mean-inglessness, a trumpeted reminder from the Church that there is indeed a plan—God's plan—and each of us has an essential place in it. Every part of the *Catechism* stresses this: from its own plan of disclosure of the content of the faith to its unremitting stress on the plan of God's provi-dence in history, the *Catechism* proclaims that nothing has been left to chance. The Father has counted the hairs of our heads and even watches the sparrow.[48]

It is a singular gift to the Church in our time that the *Catechism* stresses the planned, ordered quality of reality. God, in the person of Jesus, reveals to us our true meaning and our ultimate destiny. This is a vital antidote for those of us who have been poisoned by the current propaganda that we have no ultimate purpose, that we are merely cosmic accidents. If such propaganda is correct, then there is nothing to count on and nothing to hope for; we are destined to ultimate chaos.

Christ, the *whole Christ*, is the antidote to the modern malady of meaninglessness, and the plan he discloses is the source of our hope in a future worth embracing. That is the message of the *Catechism* because it is the message at the very heart of the Gospel. One of the most attractive elements of early Christianity was its infectious excitement over the revelation that Jesus is the Word of God, the *Logos*. He is the very Wisdom of God and the principle of order in the created universe. What the best of Greek philosophy had sought for centuries, wisdom, God has presented to man as a gift. In Christ, the purpose, reason, goal, and meaning of the whole of creation—its plan—is present with us. That is really what "*Logos*" means. Christ is in himself the thing that the best of the philosophers had sought. He is the satisfaction of every intellectual

---

[48] Luke 12:6-7.

quest, the answer to every question, the fulfillment of every human longing.

This is no less the Good News of Jesus Christ than is the fact that he has saved us from sin and death. He doesn't just save us *from* hell; he saves us *for* the beatitude of knowing him and all things in him. That is, he doesn't just save us from the eternal state of damnation but from the hell of the modern malady of meaninglessness. This is partly what St. Paul means in Romans 12:2 by exhorting us to "be transformed by the renewal of your mind, that you may prove what is the will of God, what is good and acceptable and perfect."

Since Christ is the "recapitulation" or summary of all things, his appearance discloses that all has been planned by a good God, who wills this transformation of mind—and more—in us. It is by a graced study of the plan of God that this transformation of mind is worked in us and the *Catechism* wants not only to remind us of that, but also to supply us with the program for that transformative study.

The Plan is Christological

Alpha		Ωmega
The Beginning	*Logos*	*The End*

Christ = the fullness of the *plan* of the Father

"Christ and His Church thus together make up the 'whole Christ.'"
(CCC 795)

The Plan is the Way

All this talk about the wisdom and plan of God and the renewal of our minds might sound somewhat abstract. It might even seem opposed to what we said previously about the journey of faith as a lived itinerary. Doesn't the journey from Blessing to Blessing require not just that we *know* where we are headed but also *how* to get there? What we have been talking about is not merely intellectual *formation* but intellectual *transformation*. The journey from Blessing to Blessing requires not just that we know where we are headed —to the Blessing—but also the way there. Jesus Christ, who is the summation of God's plan for us, *is* the Way.

We have to know how God intends to save us in Christ. It can fill us with hope to know that God is in control, that he has a plan, but we also have to cede control of our lives to him in accord with his plan. If we are spiritual creatures, embodied spirits, then one of the aspects of our total transformation will necessarily be intellectual. Without that new form of knowing we call faith, we would be just as rudderless as we were before. But faith has to lead us to live our lives in a different way or it is going to be what St. James called a dead faith.[49] Again, it's not enough merely to know where we are going, we have to know how to get there.

The Plan involves a Visible Church

The "how" has already been hinted at. Christ is the Way. And the "whole Christ," as the *Catechism* tells us, consists of Christ as Head together with the Church as his Body. As the *Catechism* says, "It is in the Church that Christ fulfills and reveals his own mystery as the purpose of God's plan: 'to unite all things in him.'"[50] Here the *Catechism* tells us that it is in the Church that Christ both reveals and fulfills that purpose. As it says in another place, "The Church is

---

[49] James 2:14-17.
[50] CCC 772.

both the means and the goal of God's plan."[51] Another way of saying this is that the Church *is* God's plan for us.

This is a particular quality of the Catholic faith to which you may not have given much thought. When St. Paul explains his mission to preach the Gospel, it is with reference to the Church: "To me ... this grace was given, to preach to the Gentiles the unsearchable riches of Christ, and to make all men see what is the *plan* of the mystery hidden for all ages in God who created all things; that through *the church* the manifold wisdom of God might now be made known."[52] The Church is a vital part of the Gospel revelation; the Gospel is not just about our own personal salvation, as we so often hear. It is that, certainly, but our salvation is both revealed in and worked out in the Church. "The Way" of Christianity is not just a way of living, it is membership in the Church. We become members of Christ's Body by being joined to him. That is why the "plan of the mystery" is "made known" "through the church." God's plan is to save us in Christ and our salvation is made known by our incorporation into the Church, his Mystical Body.

Even Catholics who know this will almost reflexively fall back to a very individualistic conception of faith, largely imbibed from a Protestant view of Christ and the Church. The *Catechism* wants to remind us that God, in his very act of saving us in Christ, unites us to him and to each other in the bonds of ecclesial communion.

The Way of the Church

God's plan is expressed in the Church through the virtue of faith. The *Catechism* states, "Faith is the theological virtue by which we believe in God and believe all that he has said and revealed to us, and that Holy Church proposes for our belief, because

---

[51] CCC 778.
[52] Ephesians 3:8-10, emphasis added.

he is truth itself."[53] It then adds, "By faith 'man freely commits his entire self to God.'"

Faith is a gift of God normally received in baptism. It is the power to believe what God has revealed and the way we commit ourselves entirely to God in love. The Church is the place where baptism, and so also faith, is received and the place from within which we live the life of faith.

As discussed, there are four pillars that comprise the *Catechism*.[54] In these four, the *Catechism* embodies this central tenet of its own teaching—that faith is not just a description of things believed, it is also a "life of faith." If faith is that virtue by which a Christian commits his entire self to God, then it must express itself in every facet of that person's life.

The *Catechism* itself does not propose to Christians merely a classroom course in Catholicism; it proposes that we undertake a Catholic life, a journey of faith. Faith can never be a veneer over our ordinary lives. To paraphrase Frank Sheed, faith does not merely see the same world that others see only with Catholic patches. It sees everything anew in light of Christ and so demands a commitment of the whole self. If faith is to move us toward the awesome Blessing that God is in himself, it must be more to us than one world view among others. It must engender in us the singular commitment necessary to undertake the journey.

Conclusion

So far, we have seen that the *Catechism* wants us to know that the Father has a plan. It is a "plan of loving goodness" that expresses the Father's intention to drawn us back to the Blessing from which we have come. That plan is expressed in its fullness in Jesus Christ, who comes in the very middle of human history as the *Logos*, a kind of map for human fulfillment. He is the pattern for all that the

---

[53] CCC 1814.
[54] CCC 14-17.

Father wills for us and will eventually effect by sending his Holy Spirit. Christ is at once the Blessing present among us and the portrait of the blessed man that the Beatitudes describe. He shows us that the plan for our happiness requires that we be as given to the Father in love as he is.

Those who accept the plan of the Father in Christ are united in bonds of faith, hope, and charity in the Church. The *Catechism* tells us the Church has been present in a mysterious way in prophecy from the beginning of time as the intended fulfillment of God's plan for the unification of the human race with him. As we find her today she is "one, holy, catholic, and apostolic," as we profess in the Creed. But the Church is also mystically united to her Savior in such a way that together they make up the "whole Christ." If Christ is the Way, then the "whole Christ" is the whole Way. It is not enough for us to believe in him. As the *Catechism* points out, Christ's mystery is the purpose of God's plan and that mystery is revealed in and to the Church.[55]

The plan he reveals is that we enter into his Body, the Church, and there express our belief in him in works of faith, hope, and love. These virtues are then expressed in a life of faithful profession, worship, moral living and prayer, the four parts of the *Catechism*. We see the *Catechism* doesn't just disclose the plan of the Father in Christ, it invites us to enter the plan of loving goodness which will lead us back to the Blessing of Trinitarian love.

The journey of faith can be long and difficult, subject to all the tests and trials that can befall a human life. It is not enough to know the plan, one must follow it. It has to take flesh in each one of us personally in time and history. We do not have to make this journey of faith alone—we are accompanied by the Church. When we surrender to faith we aren't simply joined to the Church of our own time, but swept up into the mammoth wave of history itself, the wave of God's sovereign will working out his plan for the

---

[55] CCC 772.

redemption and salvation of the human race in time. This working out of God's plan in time is called "the economy of salvation," to which we now turn our attention.

The Plan in the *Catechism*:
A Sampler of Texts

Pillar 1 – Creed

CCC 50: "Through an utterly free decision, God has revealed himself and given himself to man. This he does by revealing the mystery, his plan of loving goodness, formed from all eternity in Christ, for the benefit of all men." (See also CCC 1, 53, 112, 235, 257, 280, 306, 521, 686, 723, 759, 772, 776, 778, 851, 1013.)

Pillar 2 – Sacraments

CCC 1066: "In the Symbol of the faith the Church confesses the mystery of the Holy Trinity and of the plan of God's "good pleasure" for all creation: the Father accomplishes the "mystery of his will" by giving his beloved Son and his Holy Spirit for the salvation of the world and for the glory of his name." (See also CCC 1079, 1138, 1665.)

Pillar 3 – Moral Life

CCC 1739: "Man's freedom is limited and fallible. In fact, man failed. He freely sinned. By refusing God's plan of love, he deceived himself and became a slave to sin." (See also CCC 1946, 2025, 2062, 2294, 2336, 2426.)

Pillar 4 – Prayer

CCC 2738: "Christian freedom is cooperation with his providence, his plan of love for men." (See also CCC 2679, 2683, 2745, 2750, 2851, 2858.)

Chapter Three

The Economy of Salvation

"We shall know the ultimate meaning of the whole work of creation and of the entire economy of salvation and understand the marvelous ways by which his Providence led everything towards its final end." (CCC 1040)

The Plan and the Economy

There is a little redundancy in considering the "economy of salvation" after "the plan." In fact, in the letter to the Ephesians, the English word "plan" is actually used to translate the Greek term *oikonomia*, the root word for "economy."[56] In one sense, God's plan *is* the *oikonomia* or, in English, the "economy" of salvation. But there is a reason for distinguishing the two.[57] Put succinctly, if the plan is the Father's *intention* to bless us by drawing us to himself, then the economy is *how* he brings that intention about in time and history.

As discussed, we are not accidents. God is in control of our destinies. Such a plan is a kind of prerequisite insight to a study of what he has actually done in history or the economy to bring that

---

[56] Ephesians 1:9-10 (RSV).
[57] "For this plan is revealed, carried out and communicated according to a wisely ordered economy whose times and dates are determined by the Father." Jean Corbon, *Wellspring of Worship*, Matthew J. O'Connell, trans. (New York: Paulist Press, 1988), 15.

plan into effect. Before we can take seriously the history that God has revealed in Scripture, we first have to recognize that the Bible is worth a serious look. In an age in which atheism has developed an almost evangelistic fervor, it is important to remind unbelievers, as well as the faithful, that the God of the Bible can rationally be shown to exist.

The Church has always held that God can be known to exist with unaided human reason.[58] It will suffice here to say that a self-existent God, one who is the source of his own existence, who is existence itself, is the only sufficient explanation for the existence of anything else. As Frank Sheed put it, God is the only possible answer to the question, "Why is there not nothing?" So the fact that there is anything like an economy is only the result of the first act in that economy: creation. It is important today that we realize that God is creator and can be demonstrated to be so.

The God who creates from nothing sustains his creation; he is the only reason his creation *continues* to exist. God doesn't just create the universe and walk away. If he did, we would return to what we are made of—nothing! So we might say that God's work of creation really never ceases. Because history is the story of persons as they continue to exist through time, the whole possibility for the unfolding of history in an economy of salvation is grounded in God's work of both creating and sustaining the universe.

This realization of God's existence, that he must exist because we both exist and continue in being, is not yet faith. But as the *Catechism* notes, "The proofs of God's existence ... can predispose one to faith and help one to see that faith is not opposed to reason."[59] Once we realize that the hopelessness bred by atheism is groundless, we can look upon what God has revealed about the economy with fresh eyes. Those who do believe in him then become very curious about the Bible. They want to see what this God who must exist has done.

---

[58] I would encourage the reader to study "Ways of Coming to Know God" in the *Catechism* at paragraphs 31 through 35.

[59] CCC 35.

To conclude that there is a God by the use of reason—and that his commitment to our preservation in being means he has a plan for us—is distinct from knowing his plan as it has been worked out in the economy of salvation. This distinguishes the plan of God from the economy of salvation, much of which is recorded in the Bible.

To put it another way, it is one thing to come to the abstract conviction that there is a God and that he *must* have a plan, and another to actually "know" him in his works. It is similar to just meeting someone with whom you later develop a close friendship. At first, he is only an acquaintance; later you may come to love him for what he is and does. It is our faith, the gift we receive at baptism, that makes us friends of God in this deeper way. Faith tells us that God exists (which we can also know by reason), but also enables us to embrace all that he has revealed to us about who he really is—and who we are in the economy.

The Plan is Disclosed in the Economy

That explains the importance of the theme of the economy of salvation in the *Catechism* and in our lives. It is through the economy that we come to actually know God. One of the first things that the working out of God's plan in the economy teaches us is that God is Good.

Recall that in the very first paragraph of the *Catechism* we read that "God, infinitely perfect and blessed in himself, in a *plan of sheer goodness* freely created man to make him share in his own blessed life." God didn't have to create us. After all, he is "infinitely perfect and blessed in himself." Perfection doesn't *need* anything else at all. And so, that he freely wills to make us and sustain us is an absolute testimony to his goodness. To paraphrase St. Bonaventure, goodness is diffusive of itself; in other words, one of the marks of goodness is that it seeks the good of others. God wills others into existence not for himself (remember, he needs nothing) but entirely for the creatures he makes.

Therefore, in God's very first act in effecting his plan in the economy—creation—the goodness of his plan is made evident. That God freely wills to make and sustain us is an absolute testimony to his goodness. Alternately, we can know that the rest of God's plan for humanity will be good because we know that God is good. Although it is consoling to know that, in theory, God *must* have a plan, and that his plan must be good because he is good, it is another to recognize how God *really has acted in history* for our good, thereby showing his love for us. This is what the economy of salvation shows us and the *Catechism* so convincingly portrays.

At many significant points, the *Catechism* refers back to the story of salvation as it explains the Faith. We read:

> The divine plan of Revelation is realized simultaneously "by deeds and words which are intrinsically bound up with each other." It involves a specific divine pedagogy: God communicates himself to man gradually. He prepares him to welcome by stages the supernatural Revelation that is to culminate in the person and mission of the incarnate Word, Jesus Christ.[60]

What we have called the economy is this staged, gradual disclosure in history of the plan of God to save us in Christ. Note, too, that it "is realized simultaneously 'by deeds and words.'" God doesn't just tell us things, he shows us. As noted previously, the Protestant view that the Bible is the sole rule of faith and that a single profession of faith is sufficient for salvation can contribute to an overly verbal understanding of God's revelation, even by Catholics.

God impacts our history in a real and direct way. He acts, often through intermediaries, in ways that affect us positively. In short, he

---

[60] CCC 53.

doesn't just speak to us; he doesn't just send us words in a book. Most of the Bible, in fact, is taken up with a recital of the economy, of narrative descriptions of events or commentaries on those events. God speaks to us *and* acts to save us, and he has been doing so since the Fall of Adam and Eve. These words and deeds are gathered up into the content of Revelation, as it is found in the written Scriptures and the Tradition of the Church.

This is why the *Catechism* makes so prominent a use of the economy of salvation: it is not just a convenient theme, but the very fabric of our relation with God and so also of the way in which the faith, which is a sharing of that relation, is to be passed on. Thus, the general editor of the *Catechism*, Cardinal Schönborn, points out that

> the First Part [of the *Catechism*] begins by explaining all the economy of Revelation, which culminates in the mystery of Christ. The Trinitarian structure of the Apostles Creed is the expression of the Trinitarian character of the divine economy ... the Second Part explicitly extends this perspective of the economy: in the age of the Church it becomes a sacramental economy.

He goes on to note that, although the economy is less prominent in the Third Part, it is still used in that section in the "articles on law and grace that more specifically address the divine dispositions to live according to God." And with regard to the fourth pillar, on prayer, he affirms that the theme of the economy "is very much present." In fact, the economy is so prominent a feature in the *Catechism* that Cardinal Schönborn calls it "a sort of *leitmotiv* running through the new *Catechism*."[61] The economy is such an important theme in the *Catechism*, because it is the working out of God's plan in Christ in history. Still more, it describes the path of the human journey, our journey of faith, through that history toward the Blessing to which Revelation

---

[61] In James P. Socias, ed., *Reflections on the Catechism of the Catholic Church* (Chicago: Midwest Theological Forum, 1993), p. 79.

points us. The economy is the full story of blessing that we enter when we embrace the faith that proposes it to us as God's plan to draw us back to himself.

As we have previously said, a traveler needs to know three things before beginning a journey: his starting point, his destination, and the best route between the two. We also noted that there is a fourth element when undertaking a journey: our reason or purpose for going. The Blessing is both our starting point and our destination, as well as the reason or purpose for our undertaking the journey. God, then, as our origin and end—and the source of our ultimate happiness—is the ultimate reason for the journey.

Now, having come to understand a bit better the plan of God and the way that this plan is put into play in time in what we call the economy of salvation, we can begin to recognize that these are the route or path we follow on our journey to God. Let's take a closer look at the path that the *Catechism* describes.

The Planner is Disclosed in the Economy

The economy consists of the "words and deeds" by which "God communicates himself to man"[62] in a saving history that effects God's plan of loving goodness. That makes the events of that history very significant, not just because they save us but because they reveal God to us. To explain why God reveals himself in history, the *Catechism* notes that "a person discloses himself in his actions, and the better we know a person, the better we understand his actions."[63] Hence, God tells us who he is by what he does.

This is the principal reason why the *Catechism* employs snippets of narration of the economy at significant points because God himself uses this "specific divine pedagogy" to communicate himself to us.[64] The Father doesn't just *tell* us that he loves us; he loves us in fact, in his-

---

[62] CCC 53.
[63] CCC 236.
[64] CCC 53.

tory, and proves his love for us. This negates the idea that God requires a kind of blind faith from his followers. The opposite is the case. He has arranged the whole of sacred history to prove to us that he is there and that he cares. His way of teaching us about himself is as concrete and accessible as the events of time and space. He comes down to meet us where we live. The *Catechism*, then, uses the economy to teach us about God because God uses the economy to teach us about himself.

God's pedagogy, or method of teaching, aims not just at telling us the generalities about himself, but the intimate details. As the *Catechism* states, "The whole history of salvation is identical with the history of the way and the means by which the one true God, Father, Son and Holy Spirit, reveals himself to men."[65] That is, the economy itself reveals God's "innermost secret," that he is an "eternal exchange of love, Father, Son and Holy Spirit, and that he has destined us to share in that exchange."[66]

The Economy is Trinitarian

We have already seen what the *Catechism* has to say about this stupendous revelation: "The mystery of the Most Holy Trinity is the central mystery of Christian faith and life. It is the mystery of God in himself. It is therefore the source of all the other mysteries of faith, the light that enlightens them."[67] Monsignor Francis Kelly, a longtime leader in the field of catechetics, has rightly called this text the "theological key" to the *Catechism*. What he means is that the whole *Catechism* has been structured around this central tenet of our faith, that God is Father, Son, and Holy Spirit.

Since the economy of salvation is also a central theme of the *Catechism*, it shouldn't surprise us, then, that the *Catechism* should go on to say in the same paragraph where it talks about the "central mystery" of the Trinity that the history of salvation is *identical* to the revelation of

---

[65] CCC 234.
[66] CCC 221.
[67] CCC 234.

God as three divine Persons. What it means by this is that God's Trinitarian revelation of himself has so impressed itself upon the economy
that the economy is itself Trinitarian in substance and form.

As we have noted, the *Catechism* is ordered in many of its parts by
threes. This can be seen primarily in the division of the Creed into sections on the three Persons of the Trinity. These parts of the Creed also
correspond to the three phases of the economy itself: *creation* (God the
Father), *redemption* (God the Son), and our *sanctification* in the Church
(God the Holy Spirit).[68] These three terms—creation, redemption, and
sanctification—encompass the whole of God's work in history from
beginning to end. And they are the central parts of our profession of
faith in the three Persons to whom these acts are attributed.

We now see why so much of the material in the *Catechism* is arranged in threes, because God's own "specific divine pedagogy," the
economy of salvation, is Trinitarian in structure. In fact, the whole of
the economy is God's way of gradually communicating this very innermost secret about himself. As the *Catechism* says, "A person discloses
himself in his actions."

The *Catechism* amplifies this point by noting that

> [t]he Fathers of the Church distinguish between the theology
> (*theologia*) and economy (*oikonomia*). "Theology" refers to the
> mystery of God's inmost life within the Blessed Trinity and
> "economy" to all the works by which God reveals himself and
> communicates his life. Through the *oikonomia* the *theologia*
> is revealed to us; but conversely, the *theologia* illuminates the
> whole *oikonomia*. God's works reveal who he is in himself; the
> mystery of his inmost being enlightens our understanding of
> all his works.[69]

The *Catechism* is telling us that the economy is not just a collec-
tion of recounted words and events but a story that is ordered and di-

---

[68] Socias, p. 79, "The Trinitarian structure of the Apostles' Creed is the expression of the Trinitarian character of the divine economy"; see also CCC 190.
[69] CCC 236.

rected by divine love. Just as lovers want those they love to know them intimately, so also God has arranged the whole of history to disclose himself to us in an intimate way. God has made himself our constant companion, not merely by the acts he performs but even in the very structure of time, which is Trinitarian, and so reveals his Tri-unity. The whole world, in its journey from Blessing to Blessing, is accompanied by God.

Faith is received and exercised in union with the Church—not just the Church of today but that Church which, in union with her Head, constitutes "the whole Christ." We aren't on this journey alone. And now we see that we are not just accompanied by the Church of every age, those now living and those who have already arrived at the Blessing toward which we still strive, but by the Most Holy Trinity as well.

Father

Holy Spirit   Son

Theologia

"...the Most Holy Trinity... the mystery of God in himself." (CCC 234)

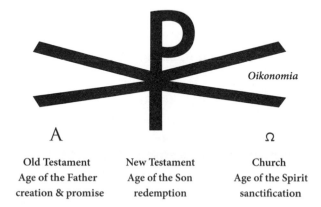

Oikonomia

A   Ω

Old Testament	New Testament	Church
Age of the Father	Age of the Son	Age of the Spirit
creation & promise	redemption	sanctification

"The whole history of salvation is identical with the history of the way and the means by which the one true God, Father, Son, and Holy Spirit, reveals himself to men 'and reconciles and unites with himself those who turn away from sin.'" (CCC 234)

The Three Act as One

An important doctrinal caveat must be inserted here. Although we can distinguish between the divine actions of creation, redemption, and sanctification and it is traditional to "appropriate" these actions to the Father, Son and Spirit, respectively, the *Catechism* reminds us that "The whole divine economy is the common work of the three divine persons."[70] "Inseparable in what they are," the *Catechism* tells us, "the divine persons are also inseparable in what they do."[71] So God has willed, as is disclosed in the missions of the Son and Spirit, to help us to understand that he is a Trinity of Persons, but a Trinity united in love, united in divinity and united in action in the economy.

Just as the Father is associated with the blessing as its Source, and just as the *plan* of blessing is associated with the Son as Logos, the working out of that plan in the economy can be associated with the Holy Spirit. It is the Holy Spirit, working with typical discretion, secretly, quietly, with what the *Catechism* calls "divine self-effacement,"[72] who sculpts the economy to prepare hearts to receive the Father's Word.

The Unique Role of the Holy Spirit

Recall that paragraph 1078 describes the Father's blessing as "both word and gift." The Father's plan is to bless us in his Son, the Word; the Spirit is the Gift that brings that plan to life in history, in the economy. Although both the Father's Word and Gift were quietly at work in the Old Testament to prepare our redemption,

---

[70] CCC 238.
[71] CCC 267. This means that, although we can say that the Father is "Creator," as we do in the Creed, or that the age of the Old Testament is the "age of the Father," all three Persons of the Trinity are at work as the one God in every divine act and in all three ages of the Old Testament, New Testament, and Church.
[72] CCC 687.

the Creed reveals that the Holy Spirit is the one who "has spoken through the prophets."[73]

The work of the Spirit in the economy is made most explicit in the *Catechism* when the economy of Old and New Testament history is shown to be mystically transformed into the sacramental economy of the Church. As the *Catechism* tells us,

> In this sacramental dispensation of the Christ's mystery the Holy Spirit acts in the same way as at other times in the economy of salvation: he prepares the Church to encounter her Lord; he recalls and makes Christ manifest to the faith of the assembly. By his transforming power, he makes the mystery of Christ present here and now. Finally the Spirit of communion unites the Church to the life and mission of Christ.[74]

To summarize, there is a Trinitarian character of the themes we have been examining. In short, the blessing of the Father, planned for in the Son, is effected in the Spirit in the two phases of the one economy: the economy of history and the sacramental mystery.

Telling the Story and the Conviction of Faith

We have seen that God's work of disclosing himself in the economy of salvation constitutes a "specific divine pedagogy." God becomes our *teacher* when we begin to pay close attention to what he has done in salvation history. The deeds and words of that economy are bound up with and shed light on each other. God prepares us gradually "to welcome by stages the supernatural Revelation that

---

[73] The Spirit's work is also made evident in paragraphs 702-741, which describe the work of the Spirit in the divine economy, in creation, in the promise to Abraham, in the Exodus and giving of the Law on Sinai, in the preparation of a remnant in Israel, in the Incarnation of Christ by the Virgin Mary, in the ministry of Christ Himself, and at Pentecost and the ensuing age of the Church.

[74] CCC 1092.

is to culminate in the person and mission of the Incarnate Word, Jesus Christ."

Those two elements, the enlightening interrelation of the deeds and words of the economy and the fact that the economy is gradual or staged, give the economy the quality of a story. What the *Catechism* has called "the plan" could also be described as "the plot." And that plot is worked out in a series of specific words and actions in the economy that are "bound up with each other and so "shed light on each other." That is just the way that the parts of a story function, too. Just as the *plot* is disclosed in the interrelated events of a *story*, so also the *plan* of God is disclosed in the interrelated events of the *economy*.

If you were given a story to read which consisted of a series of unrelated events, you would conclude that it had no plot. "One thing didn't lead to the next," you might rightly complain. You might even say that it wasn't a story at all. The "modern malady of meaningless" comes from this sense that there is no plot to our life stories, that life isn't a story at all. The interrelation of events in the economy—the plan or story of salvation history—are so majestically interrelated that when we hear it told we are left with a profound sense of the beauty and harmony of the plan as it is fulfilled in the economy. In literary terms, the tightness of its plot shows us that God is a supremely artful storyteller.

If that profound sense of the plan's beauty and harmony is rare among Christians, that is perhaps because the proper telling of this divine story is rarer still. So along with insisting that there is a plan, the *Catechism* takes time to tell the story wherever it seems warranted. In doing so, it is reviving the ancient catechetical practice of narration, in Latin *narratio*, that so effectively worked in the first

Christian centuries in forming the kind of Christians who could face the lions of Rome.

As St. Irenaeus put it near the end of the second century A.D., "Faith is established upon things truly real, that we may believe what really is, as it is, and [believing] what really is, as it is, we may always keep our conviction of it firm."[75] That is, a firm grasp of the story of salvation, which is *the* true story, yields not just faith, but the *conviction* of faith. Today we need convicted Christians who can face the lions of our own age and the *Catechism* wants to arm us with the conviction that this true story provides.

A Sacramental Story

This best of stories by the best of storytellers is divinely artful. It can seem that one thing leads to another in ways that are too good to be true. This is because God can, even while utilizing free human agents, "write" history so that it reveals himself and his love in surprising ways. Without negating free will, God the Holy Spirit directed the plan that unfolds in the Old Testament in such a way "that it should prepare for and declare in prophecy the coming of Christ, redeemer of all men."[76] God wrote a story that from the beginning planned on Christ as the hero who arrives just in time to save us. And the "happily ever after" in this story is the marriage between Christ and his Church in the sacraments. As the *Catechism* puts it, "In this age of the Church Christ now lives and acts in and with his Church, in a new way appropriate to this new age. He acts through the sacraments in what the common Tradition calls 'the sacramental economy'."[77]

The Old Testament economy that prepares for and yields Christ in the economy of the New Testament passes into the sacramental economy of the Church. In the age of the Church the two

---

[75] St. Irenaeus of Lyon, *On the Apostolic Preaching.*
[76] CCC 122.
[77] CCC 1076.

older phases of the economy are recalled and made present in our lives through the mysterious agency of the sacramental actions. In this way the story is ongoing. While the public revelation that we receive in the Bible and Tradition is closed,[78] the fruits of the full-ness of that revelation which are found in Christ are still applied in the midst of our individual stories in the graces we receive from the sacramental re-presentation of the great works of God in the economy. Those fruits unite our personal stories to the grand story that will continue until all the blessed are gathered into the Father's house at the end of time.

It is the gift of faith that enables us to see the marvelously unified and purposeful plan of God as disclosed in the economy of salvation. "The grace of faith opens 'the eyes of your hearts,'" the *Catechism* tells us, "to a lively understanding of the contents of Revelation: that is, of the totality of God's plan and the mysteries of faith, of their connection with each other and with Christ, the center of the revealed mystery."[79]

Our Response in Faith

Through the arrangement of the four pillars of the *Catechism*, the Church shows us that just as God reveals himself in words and deeds in the economy of salvation, we are to respond in words and deeds in our lives. This response of faith includes not just a profes-sion of what we believe; it is also expressed in celebration or litur-gical worship, adherence to the moral law, and personal prayer. In Romans 2:13, we read that "it is not the hearers of the law who are righteous before God, but the doers of the law who will be justified."

This "doing" means that our journey of faith will be creedal, sacramental, moral, and orational—made up of the profession of faith, worship, right living and prayer. Those four, like the rungs of a ladder, enable us to ascend to the Blessing by way of a trinity of gifts:

---

[78] See CCC 66.
[79] CCC 158.

faith, hope and charity. We express our faith in the creed, our hope is expressed and enlivened in the sacraments, and we love God and neighbor by living a virtuous life and through prayer. Those virtues perfect the trinity of powers in us: faith perfects the intellect, hope the memory, and love the will.

What this shows us is that our personal economy of salvation is no less Trinitarian than the larger, world economy in which God creates, redeems and seeks to sanctify the human race. And that Trinitarian economy of personal salvation is intended to be the map for our way home to the Blessing from which we come.

The economy is not just a series of events that we study from a distance. The ancient economy is "continued in the mission of the Church."[80] Those past events of creation, redemption, and sanctification are professed in the Creed, but those events are also mystically made present in the "sacramental economy" in the Church's ongoing life of worship.[81]

The economy of the three ages of natural law, Old Law, and New Law is still being played out in our personal moral struggle to come into conformity with the picture of the Beatitudes that Christ is in himself. And the "covenant drama of prayer … which unfolds throughout the whole history of salvation"[82] must also be lived at its depths in our own personal journey of faith. That happens when the blessings of that saving history that the narration of the economy makes known to the believer become the very matter of his or her prayer. "Because God blesses, the human heart can in return bless the One who is the source of every blessing."[83] When we do that, we imitate Mary who "pondered" all the wonderful things that God had done in her heart and praised him in that song we call her

---

[80] CCC 257.
[81] CCC 1076.
[82] CCC 2567.
[83] CCC 2626.

Magnificat: "He who is mighty has done great things for me, and holy is his name."[84]

Conclusion: Jacob's Ladder

The *Catechism* gives a kind of summary of the purpose of God's plan to lead us into the eternal Blessing that he is: "The ultimate end of the whole divine economy is the entry of God's creatures into the perfect unity of the Blessed Trinity."[85] This movement from Blessing to Blessing which the *Catechism* maps out for each of us is ordered to our recognition that we are part of this larger journey of the Trinitarian stages of the economy of salvation history. In the process, our personal history becomes a salvation history. Our story is inserted into the world's story; our lives enter into the stream of this mammoth movement of the whole of history which has come forth from the eternal Blessing and which is headed back to it again. This is the epic journey upon which the whole of the cosmos has been embarked since it came forth from the open hand of the good God at the beginning of time.

The *Catechism's* four pillars are not just foundations of the Christian life, and still less are they mere categories of doctrinal content. They are best thought of as four rungs on the ladder of ascent back to the Father. Jesus gave us that image when he said "Truly, truly, I say to you, you will see heaven opened, and the angels of God ascending and descending upon the Son of man."[86] That gospel image is a fulfillment of the vision of the House of God (the Church) that the patriarch Jacob had at Bethel where he saw "a ladder set up on the earth, and the top of it reached to heaven."[87]

These four major rungs represent many smaller rungs as well. The first pillar covers the twelve articles of the Apostles' Creed. These articles can be thought of as twelve rungs by which we climb

---

[84] Luke 1:49; see also 2:19 and 2:51.

[85] CCC 260.

[86] John 1:51.

[87] John 28:12.

higher and higher in approaching the Mystery of God. They begin with the Father's work of creation at the beginning of time and end with "life everlasting."

In the second pillar, we step up onto the seven rungs of the sacraments, which give us a foretaste of that final destination and which enable us by grace to ascend to the eight rungs of the Beatitudes, the ten rungs of the Commandments, and the seven rungs of prayer, which are represented by the seven petitions of the Our Father.

That gives us a clearer picture of what the *Catechism* is about. Out of its three major themes of blessing, plan, and economy we have teased out the starting point and destination of the Christian journey, well as its purpose and path. And what we have found in it is the prophesied ladder of ascent that God promised to Jacob and fulfilled in Christ. It rises up now in front of us with its feet on the earth and its upper reaches in the heavens. It's now up to us to put a foot up on the first rung, to take up the Christian journey that the *Catechism* proposes with renewed vigor and commitment...and to climb.

Whether or not we choose to undertake that journey into the Blessing that patiently waits for us is the central issue of our lives and determines whether we will be, as C.S. Lewis puts it, eternal splendors or everlasting horrors. The material world is already on a journey toward its end. We, on the other hand, will have no end. Our *journey* ends in an eternal Sabbath of blessed rest, but it is not the end of us. Our journey's end is the end for which we were created: the graced happiness that comes in the blessed vision of the God who created, redeemed, and will sanctify us ... if only we are willing to undertake the journey from Blessing to Blessing.

The Journey from Blessing to Blessing

CCC#1 "God infinitely perfect
and *blessed* in himself...

...in a *plan* of sheer goodness...

Father

Holy Spirit   Son

freely created man...   ...to make him share in his own blessed life."

    ↓   ↑ *Prayer* – blessing received and given

    ↓   ↑ *Moral life* – fulfillment in beatitude

    ↓   ↑ *Sacraments* – the blessing revealed & given

    ↓   ↑ *Creed* – story of the plan of blessing in miniature

Economy   →   ☨   → The Church & her life of Faith
of Salvation

Jesus Christ   ↑ The Journey or Ladder in
[the Father's plan revealed]   the *Catechism*

Memory

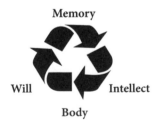

Will   Intellect   CCC#27 "The desire for God
                                           is written in the human
Body   heart....Only in God will
                                           he find the truth & *happiness*
                                           he never stops searching for."

The Concept of "Economy" in the *Catechism*: A Sampler of Texts

Pillar 1 – Creed

CCC 122: "Indeed, "the economy of the Old Testament was deliberately so oriented that it should prepare for and declare in prophecy the coming of Christ, redeemer of all men." (See also CCC 56, 66, 236, 258, 705, 1040.)

Pillar 2 – Sacraments

CCC 1093: "In the sacramental economy the Holy Spirit fulfills what was prefigured in the Old Covenant." (See also CCC 1066, 1076, 1168, 2131.)

Pillar 3 – Moral Life

CCC 2541: "The economy of law and grace turns men's hearts away from avarice and envy. It initiates them into desire for the Sovereign Good; it instructs them in the desires of the Holy Spirit who satisfies man's heart." (See also CCC 1739, 2131.)

Pillar 4 – Prayer

CCC 2738: "The revelation of prayer in the economy of salvation teaches us that faith rests on God's action in history." (See also CCC 2641, 2651, 2666, 2746, 2808, 2850.)

About the Author

Dr. Sean Innerst teaches theology and catechetics at St. John Vianney Theological Seminary and the Augustine Institute in Denver, where he resides with his wife, Cathy, and their five children. The catechetical principles outlined in *From Blessing to Blessing* are those which Sean has employed in his adult education classes and his work in training future pastors and catechists.